TE

POPULAR INSTRUMENTAL HITS

Project Manager: Tony Esposito
Book Design: Jorge Paredes

© 1997 WARNER BROS. PUBLICATIONS
All Rights Reserved

ANGEL EYES

Composed by
JIM BRICKMAN

Angel Eyes - 2 - 1
IF9707

TIJUANA TAXI

Music by
ERVAN F. COLEMAN

IF9707

RISE

By
ANDY ARMER and
RANDY BADAZZ

CUTE

Music by
NEAL HEFTI

IF9707

EBB TIDE

Lyric by
CARL SIGMAN

Music by
ROBERT MAXWELL

IF9707

SPANISH FLEA

By
JULIUS WECHTER

ST. LOUIS BLUES

Words and Music by
W.C. HANDY

Slow blues

THE ENTERTAINER

By
SCOTT JOPLIN

The Entertainer - 2 - 1
IF9707

Coda

D.S. % al Coda

EUROPA
(Earth's Cry Heaven's Smile)

By
CARLOS SANTANA
and TOM COSTER

Moderately slow

TAKE FIVE

By
PAUL DESMOND

rit. e dim.

IF9707

THE SWINGIN' SHEPHERD BLUES

Words by
RHODA ROBERTS and KENNY JACOBSON

Music by
MOE KOFFMAN

IF9707

GREEN ONIONS

Music by
BOOKER T. JONES, STEVE CROPPER,
LEWIS STEINBERG and AL JACKSON, JR.

HOLIDAY FOR STRINGS

Words by
SAMMY GALLOP

Music by
DAVID ROSE

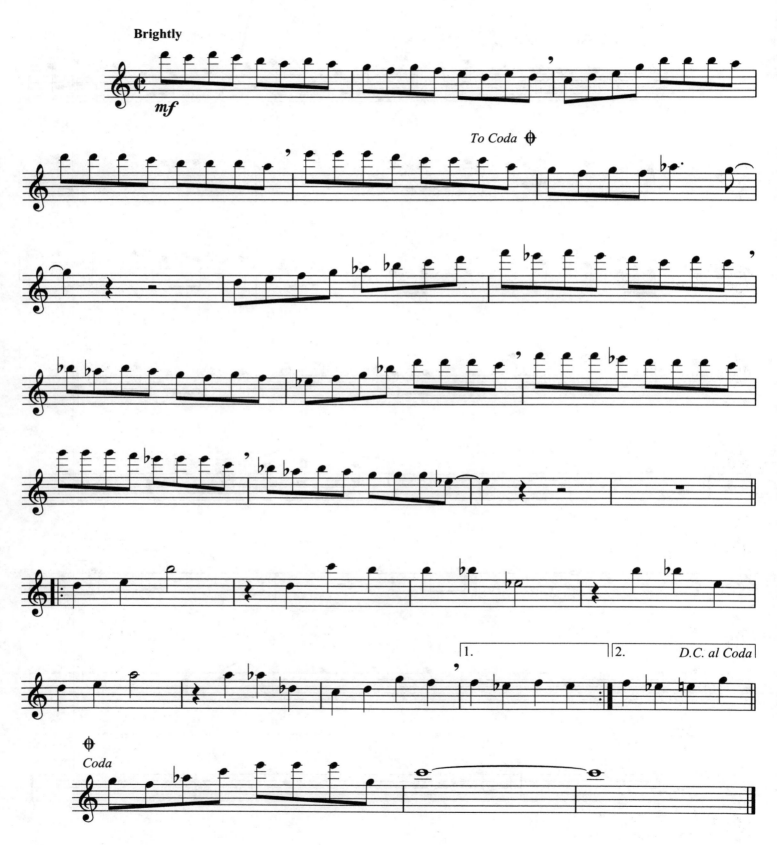

IF9707

THE PINK PANTHER

Music by
HENRY MANCINI

IF9707

THE HUSTLE

By
VAN McCOY

Moderately fast

THE MASTERPIECE
(Theme from "Masterpiece Theatre")

By
J.J. MOURNET
and PAUL PARNES

IF9707

THEME FROM ICE CASTLES
(Through the Eyes of Love)

Lyrics by
CAROLE BAYER SAGER

Music by
MARVIN HAMLISCH

LOVE THEME FROM ST. ELMO'S FIRE
(Instrumental)

By
DAVID FOSTER

INSPECTOR CLOUSEAU THEME

By
HENRY MANCINI

THE LONELY BULL
(El Solo Toro)

Music by
SOL LAKE

IF9707

L.A. LAW
Main Title

By
MIKE POST

IF9707

LINUS AND LUCY

By
VINCE GUARALDI

IF9707

LAST DATE

By
FLOYD CRAMER

LI'L DARLIN'

By
NEAL HEFTI

IF9707

LAST TANGO IN PARIS

By
GATO BARBIERI